THE SPICE OF LIFE

Michaela Morgan
Rosalind Kerven
Anthony Masters

THE SPICE OF LIFE

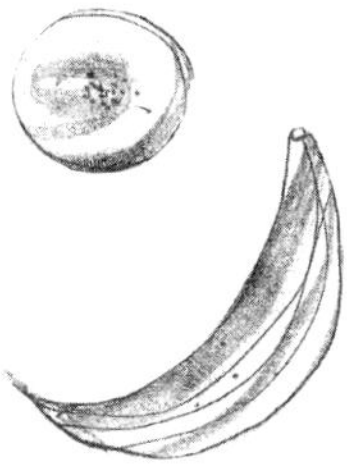

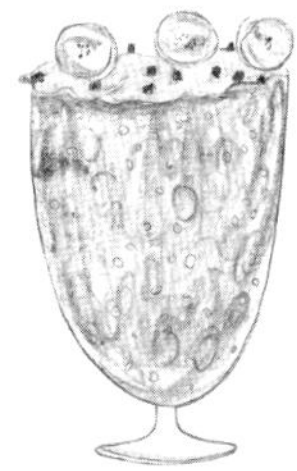

Contents

Banana Smoothie!

Anansi the spider liked nothing better than lazing around. It drove his poor spouse completely bananas! Anansi would find a patch of sunlight, settle down, close his eyes, and let his head fill with dreams and cunning schemes. Meanwhile, his wife laundered and minded the children, prepared and cooked their food, and fed them. The children helped out as much as they were able – but Anansi did nothing.

Today was no different. Anansi was lying back, dozing and dreaming when ...

"WAAAAAAAH!" went his youngest child.

And "WAAAAAAAAAAAH!" went his middle child.

And "WAAAAAAAAAAAAAAAAAAAAAAAH!" went his eldest child.

Then in unison they cried, "WE'RE HUNGRY!"

"I feel a bit peckish myself," Anansi murmured sleepily. "Wife! What about some nourishment?"

"What about some nourishment indeed!" she replied. "Take a look!"

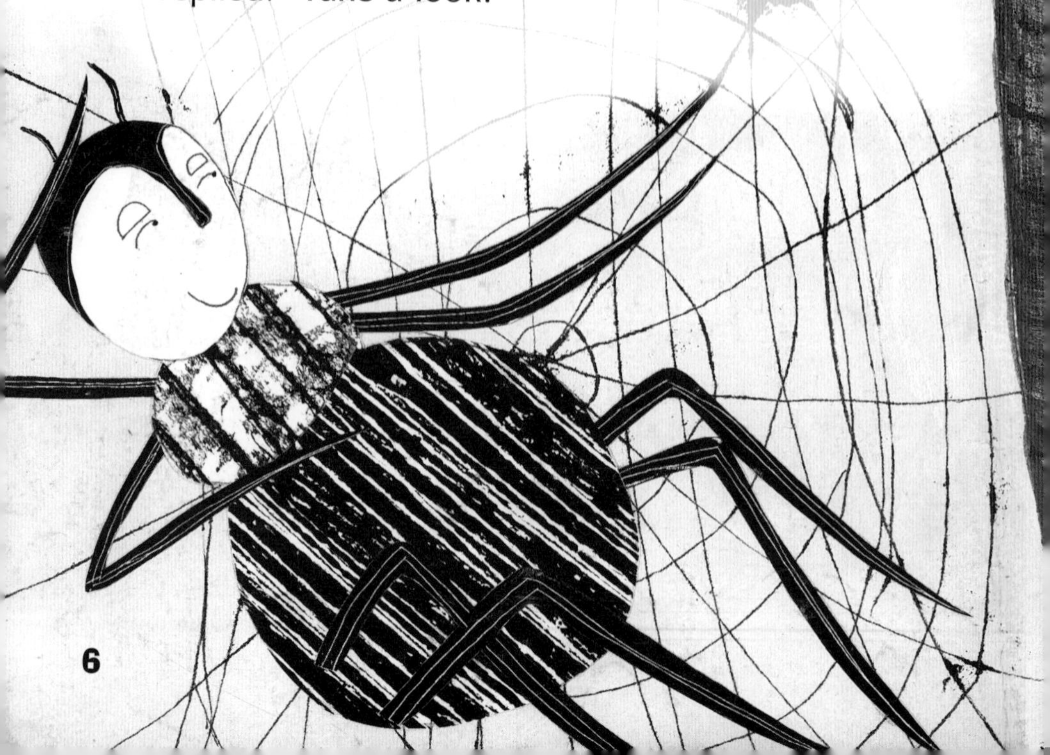

She opened the larder door and revealed the contents: a few berries (past their best), some nuts (a bit shrivelled), a jug of milk (rather small), the scrapings at the base of a honeypot, and an old sock (how did that get there?).

"How am I to feed a family of five on that?" she demanded.

Anansi gazed at her through half-closed eyes, and offered her his most charming smile. "Oh, you can do anything ..." he drawled. "You are such a clever creature ... such a wonderful wife ... such a marvellous mother ..."

Anansi was a charmer. He got what he wanted through a mix of charm and smarm and downright lies. He was a smoothie all right!

But his wife was accustomed to his ways and would not be distracted by his flattery. "Up you get and out you go!" she insisted. "It's up to you to go out to get us some food. Go and find some work. *Earn* some food."

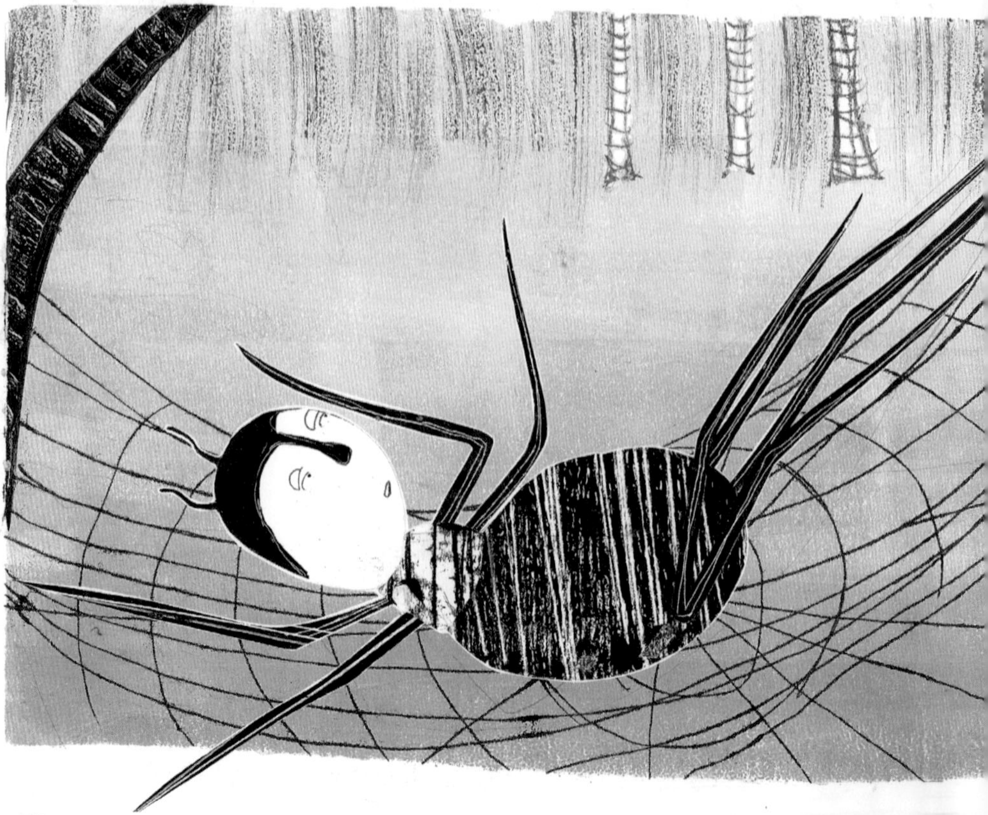

Anansi yawned and stretched. His wife got hold of his outstretched legs and yanked at him.

"Up you get and out you go! You crafty, cunning, lazy, good-for-nothing, sneaky, scheming ..."

Anansi sighed. *I'll get no peace here,* he thought to himself. *I'll just wander in the woods and fields for a while, and return when she's calmed down ...*

but before he could finish his lazy little plan, his wife had added, "... and don't come back until you can feed your family."

Now this was serious! Anansi liked his home comforts. *The woods are wild at night,* he thought, *and chilly too! And I certainly don't want to work. Work always makes me feel so exhausted. I think I might be allergic to it.*

He wandered through the fields. There was plenty of work to be had. All around him his friends and neighbours were ploughing and planting, growing and gathering. The fields were full of peas and sweet potatoes, beans and coconuts, pineapples and bananas – but they were all jealously guarded by the farmers.

“You can do some digging for me,” said one.

“But I’d get a bad back,” moaned Anansi.

“You can climb my trees to gather coconuts,” said another.

“I’d get a dizzy head,” said Anansi.

“You can plant some peas for me,” said a third.

“My feet would ache,” replied Anansi, and he sat down to rest under the shade of a palm tree.

Down the road came his friend the rat. Ratso was carrying an enormous bunch of bananas on his head. He tried to scurry past Anansi, but Anansi flashed his most winning smile. The charm offensive had started ...

"My oh my! That's a fine bunch of bananas you have, my friend," Anansi flattered.

"Thanks," said Ratso, and tried to hurry on.

"I think they're the finest I've seen this year," said Anansi smoothly. "Did you grow them yourself?"

"I did," the rat admitted proudly. "They're the best I've ever grown."

“You are obviously a farmer of talent,” Anansi said charmingly. “Everyone who looks at your bunch of bananas will see you are the most successful farmer around!”

“Why, thank you!” Ratso blushed.

“They are so well formed, so well coloured, so perfect – well, almost perfect.”

“Almost?” Ratso looked anxiously at his bunch of bananas. “Only almost perfect?”

“Yes, my friend,” Anansi continued. “There are a few in the bunch that are ruining the look. They will lose you your reputation too if you’re not careful.”

Ratso peered at his bunch of bananas.

"You see ..." said Anansi, frowning at the bananas, "that one is spotted. Not that a spotted banana is a bad thing. Indeed, my wife prefers them to all others – but it doesn't look as good as the others, does it?"

Ratso looked at the banana doubtfully.

"If I were you, I'd take it off the bunch," advised Anansi.

Ratso snapped the banana off the bunch. "Give it to your wife," said the generous rat. "She's always been very kind to me."

"I'll take it off your hands," Anansi offered. "And while you're tidying the bunch, have a think about that one – it has a brown patch just at the tip. Of course, a brown tip can mean the banana is extra sweet and my eldest child loves the sweetest bananas, but it doesn't look good does it?"

Ratso thought for a moment and snapped the banana off the bunch. "Give this to your eldest," he said. "He helped me out last week."

"Ah, I always said you were a fair and generous rat," purred Anansi. "A fair rat! A fine rat! And one with such a great sense of humour. I know that you will enjoy it when everyone laughs at that strangely shaped banana in your bunch."

"Which one is that?" asked the worried rat.

"That one with the blobby lumps," said Anansi. "How my middle child would chuckle at that one."

Ratso gave the banana to Anansi. "Give it to your middle child," he said. "She's a good, obedient child, and she deserves good things."

"Why, you really are the kindest rat in the whole wide world!" Anansi gushed. "Perhaps you could spare that little green banana – for my baby you know. It wouldn't be kind to leave the baby out, and that banana is the perfect size for a baby."

"Very well," said Ratso, and he gave the small green banana to Anansi.

So now Anansi had one small green banana, one lumpy odd-looking banana, one brown-tipped banana and one spotty banana. He had one for everyone in his family – except himself.

"What about a banana for your old friend Anansi?" he wheedled.

But Ratso would only be pushed so far. "My bunch looks very tidy now, thank you very much," he said firmly. "I admire your wife and I love your children but when have *you* ever been a friend to me? When have *you* ever helped me out? Never!" With that, the rat scurried away.

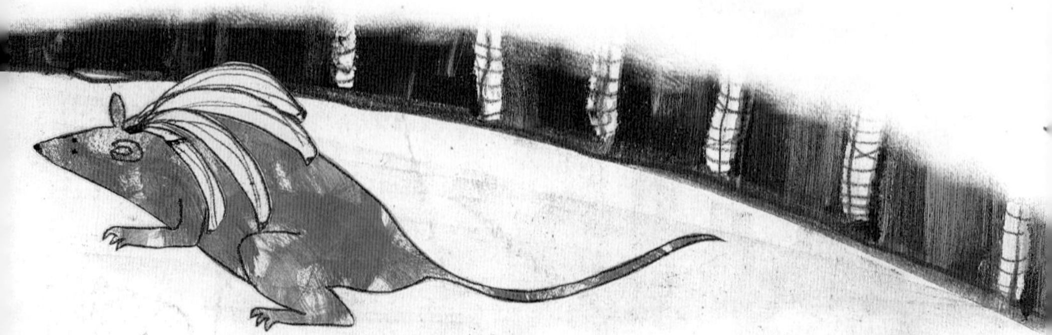

"Rats! Rats! RATS!" cried Anansi. "And I love bananas too!" He sighed, picked up his bananas and set off for home.

When Anansi arrived home, his family came running out to greet him.

"Look what I've got for you!" Anansi announced and gave his wife a kiss. "Look what your handsome husband has for you. Lovely bananas. Such special bananas too. I chose each one so carefully. A spotted banana for my dear wife, a tiny green banana for the baby, a funny lumpy one and a sweet brown-tipped one. Special bananas for my special family. Haven't I done well?"

His children were delighted, and even his wife seemed almost impressed.

"You did well to earn them so quickly," she sniffed.

Anansi smiled weakly and sank down onto his bed. "I have worked my fingers to the bone," he moaned. "My back aches, my head hurts, and my feet are burning and swollen, but I did it all for you, my loved ones.

"So do not worry, beloved wife, do not fret, darling children. It matters not that there is no banana for me." He closed his eyes wearily. "I'm too worn out to eat anyway. Just leave me here, go off and enjoy your bananas ..." His bottom lip quivered and he rested his hands on his stomach.

The children had started peeling their bananas, but now they stopped and stared at Anansi.

The middle child sobbed. "Poor Daddy," she said. "Have half of my banana."

"You can have half of mine, I suppose," sighed his wife.

"And half of mine!" squeaked the baby.

"And half of mine," said the eldest child.

So Anansi's family had half a banana each and Anansi had half his middle child's, half his wife's, half his baby's,.and half his eldest child's. Anansi felt very pleased with himself. He was just about to scoff two bananas in all when ...

"Stop! Not so quick!" cried his wife. She grabbed back all the bananas and put them in a bowl. She had realised Anansi's plan.

"Oh cunning! Cunning!" she said. "You were going to wolf down all those bananas and leave us with just half each. That's not fair shares! You cunning, conniving, crafty, greedy, lazy old ..." she muttered (and a lot worse besides).

"Have you got a better plan then?" sneered Anansi. "Do you know a way to share these few bananas between us?"

"I do!" Mrs A announced proudly and she went to get her cookery book.

This is what she found:

Banana Smoothie

for 2 servings

* 1 banana
* 1/2 cup of yoghurt or milk
* berries to taste (optional)

This recipe is particularly good for using spotty bananas.

* Peel the banana.
* Slice into chunks and place in a sealable bag.
* Wash and stem the berries (if used) and place them in the same bag.
* Seal the bag and freeze for up to three hours. (If you do not have time to freeze the fruit, just add ice cubes to the final mixture.)
* Place the frozen fruit in a blender. (If they are frozen too solid, defrost slightly.)
* Add the milk and blend until the mixture is smooth and thick.

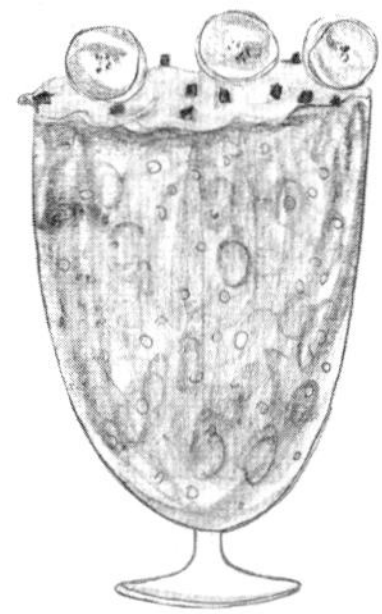

* Pour into a bowl and serve immediately with spoons.
* Honey, chocolate, nuts, sprinkles, slices of lime, slices of banana, sugar, etc. can be used for decoration.
* Non-fat yoghurt or soya milk can be used.

"That's it!" she cried. "It's a banana smoothie for us. It will last longer (half a banana would have gone in a gulp). It will be nourishing. It will use up all the scraps in my larder (except for the old sock – and I still don't know how that got there). And there will be lots and lots of it – enough for all of us."

She got to work and soon each member of her family had a delicious banana smoothie in front of them. Each of them sprinkled the top of their smoothie with a different topping. One had nuts, one had a slice of banana, one had a few berries, one had a drizzle of honey. The only thing left in the larder was the old sock. And nobody wanted that!

"Delicious, my dear!" smiled Anansi, and he licked his lips.

"Yummy!" said the eldest child, licking out his glass.

"Scrummy!" said the middle child, licking her nose.

"Goo-goo-gooood!" said the baby, licking his face and his feet – the smoothie had gone everywhere, and it was too good to waste.

"Brilliant!" said Anansi's wife. She giggled to herself. "And particularly perfect for that husband of mine because he does drive me bananas – and as I'm sure you'll agree, he is such a smoothie!"

Trolls' Porridge

There was once a boy who lived on the edge of the forest with his father and two elder brothers. The father laboured all day long and much of the night too, and one day he got into a terrible rage.

"Why don't you boys ever do anything to help?" he shouted. "Have you looked in the woodshed recently? It's almost empty. Unless one of you goes into the forest *immediately* to chop some more wood, the fire that keeps this whole house warm is going to go out and we'll all freeze to death. Then you'll be sorry!"

"I'll go and chop some firewood," offered the boy at once.

"I didn't mean *you*," said the father scornfully. "You're such a little weakling, you'd take all day just to chop one log." He turned to his eldest son and yelled, "Hey, it's you that I'm looking at!"

The eldest brother tried to wriggle out of it with excuses; but the father went on and on at him, until he hauled himself out of his chair and went grumbling out into the snow.

In less than an hour he was back, looking as white as snow himself. "I'm not going out there again!" he cried. "The whole forest is full of trolls."

"Rubbish," said the father. "What a pathetic excuse to get out of doing a job!"

But the youngest boy said: "Trolls? What are they?"

The eldest brother went and squatted beside him. "Trolls are monsters," he said. "They live in caves full of treasure. They're as big as giants, uglier even than you are – and they're very, very nasty."

"I'd like to see one," said the boy.

"You wouldn't like the one *I* saw," said the eldest brother.

"Why? What did it do?"

The eldest brother shivered. "It leapt out and grabbed me with its filthy claws. Then it yelled in my ear that if I dared chop down even one tiny tree, it would chop off my head and gobble me up for its dinner!"

"Don't be ridiculous!" said the father. "Trolls aren't real. No one believes in such things nowadays. Now, what about this wood for the fire?"

"I'll fetch some," repeated the youngest boy.

"Not you," snapped the father. "You're not strong enough to swing the axe. Besides, the forest is thick and the snow is deep; you're bound to get lost."

He turned to the middle brother. "Come on, it's your turn. Get up, get out and mind you bring back a big bundle of wood before dark."

Well, the middle brother couldn't get out of it. But he was soon back too – in a terrible sweat, with his teeth chattering and all out of breath.

"I've seen it!" he gasped. "It's really true! I saw the troll. It's horrible! It's dreadful! It's a nightmare!"

The father ranted and raved and threatened. Still he couldn't get either of the two older brothers to go out again.

Still the youngest boy kept saying, "I'll go! I'll go!"

The other two burst out laughing. "You? You're so short, you can't even see over the top of a tree stump!"

"You're so puny, all you could do is scratch at the wood with a tiny kitchen knife!"

"I'll show you," said the youngest boy. "At least I'm not a coward like you two."

He went to the store cupboard, fetched a whole soft cheese, wrapped it in a cloth and put it in his backpack. He dropped the axe in beside it, swung the whole lot onto his back, and crept out into the icy air.

Whistling, he trudged out of the garden gate, up the mountainside and into the forest. The snow was hard, bumpy and difficult to walk on. Even so, the boy made the best of it.

It was very silent, still and gloomy. Huge icicles and dead, crumbling toadstools hung from all the trees.

The boy plodded on, peering anxiously about him.

Eventually he came to a clearing of tree stumps scattered with sawdust. This was the place where his father usually came to chop wood. He walked into the middle of the clearing, stopped and looked around.

Nothing happened.

He pulled the axe from his bag. It certainly was very heavy; but he managed to swing it back and ram it hard into one of the tree stumps with a loud THUD!

The next minute there was a great crashing and thrashing through the trees at the opposite edge of the clearing – and out jumped a troll!

It was as big as four men, with a wobbling belly, stained teeth and a broken potato-nose. Its huge fists punched at the air like a drunken boxer, and its words tumbled out like vomit.

"Go away!" it shouted. "Scram! This is my forest, you little dung-beetle, and if you dare touch one of my trees, I'll tear you to shreds!"

The boy's heart was going thump-thump-thump and his knees were shaking so badly, he could hardly stand. But he didn't let his fear show. Instead, he sat down on the nearest tree stump and opened his backpack. Then, trying very hard to look calm, he took out the cheese.

He didn't dare look up; but he could feel the ground shaking as the troll came stomping closer.

"What are you doing?" it sneered.

The boy swallowed. He cleared his throat. Trying to keep his voice steady, he said, "Watch ... watch this."

The troll came so close that the boy could smell the stale stench of its breath. The boy unwrapped the cheese and held it up, but he didn't eat it.

The troll put its potato-nose right up to it and sniffed. "What's that?"

"What ... what does it look like?" stammered the boy. "It ... it's a stone. Look, I'm going to show you a trick."

He gave the cheese a good, hard squeeze. Slowly, it squashed up and a trickle of milky liquid came oozing out.

"Cor!" said the troll, "you just squeezed milk out of that stone! I've never seen that done before. You must be really strong!"

"Oh, I am," said the boy. He wasn't shaking so badly now. "I'm just as strong as you are, Mr Troll, so don't you go fighting me."

The troll stared at him. It stared at the squashed cheese. "I was only joking before," it smirked. "We're friends, aren't we?" Then suddenly it flung a great, hairy arm tightly around the boy's shoulders.

"Get off!" said the boy; but the troll only clung on to him tighter and tighter.

"Come back to my cave, my friend," said the troll. It winked. "We could have something to eat and play some games together."

"No thanks," said the boy, trying to wriggle away; but suddenly the troll dug in its claws, twirled the boy around, and dragged him into the trees!

The troll made the boy walk for hours and hours. They went up and up the mountain, deeper and deeper into the snow-covered forest. Night fell and it grew even colder. At long last, they stopped in front of a huge gaping cave.

"This is where I live," said the troll. It grabbed the boy's wrist and dragged him inside.

The cave was lit by flaming torches. Everything inside it was made of stone. There was a stone bed, a rickety stone table and two stone chairs. The walls were dripping with water and mould. The floor was covered with bones, rotting cabbage stalks and other disgusting rubbish.

Right at the back of the cave there was an enormous wooden chest. Its lid was open and the boy could see it was filled with something that glittered and gleamed through the shadows.

Treasure!

There were piles of gold nuggets. There was row after row of sparkling silver bars. There were diamonds, emeralds, rubies and sapphires. There were heaps of rings, necklaces and all kinds of other precious jewels.

The boy's eyes almost popped out of his head.

"Don't you dare touch my things!" snapped the troll. "Come on, come into the kitchen. We'll boil up some porridge."

"But I hate porridge," said the boy.

"Oh, you'll love Trolls' Porridge!" said the troll. It licked its chops with a rough, yellow tongue. "It's much tastier than the human sort. I'll show you how to make it."

The troll led the boy into a corner of the cave where there was a deep stone sink and an iron stove. It found a rusty cauldron and placed it on top of the stove. Then it pulled a stone jar off a shelf and opened the lid. The jar was full to the brim with oats.

The troll gave the boy a huge metal cup. "Let's get cooking," it said. "Scoop up ten cups full of oats, boy, and put them into this cauldron."

The boy couldn't see any way out of it, so he did exactly as he was told.

The troll went to the stone sink and turned on the tap. "Add twenty cups of water to the cauldron," said the troll.

And the trembling boy did.

The troll began to dribble with excitement. The boy felt sick and tried to dodge out of the way, but the troll shoved a big wooden spoon into his hand and told him to stir the water into the oats.

As soon as they were well mixed, the troll lit the stove. In no time at all, the porridge was coming to the boil.

"Now for the fun part!" said the troll. It reached up to a high shelf and pulled down lots of small, dark jars.

"Cinnamon!" it cried, opening the first jar and tipping a big sprinkle of brown powder into the porridge. "Ginger!" and it tipped in some yellowish powder from another jar. "Raisins! Coconut!" it shouted as a stream of black and white bits went raining down into the porridge. "Stir it, boy, stir it! Mix it all up!"

Soon even the boy had to admit it smelt quite delicious. He stirred the porridge furiously, and the troll grabbed another spoon and stirred with him.

"It's almost done," said the troll. "Now, let's just make it nice and creamy." He found a bowl of yoghurt, poured in a big dollop and stirred it round and round. "There! It's finished!"

The troll pointed across the cave to the table. "Go and sit down, boy. Are you ready for the eating match?"

"Eating match?" gulped the boy. "Er, what's that?"

"Don't you know?" said the troll. "It's a famous old troll custom at mealtimes. We have a race to see who's quickest at guzzling the porridge down."

Nervously, the boy went to sit at the table. The troll filled two enormous bowls with the porridge, carried them to the table and banged them down with a spoon beside each one. Then it sat down opposite the boy.

"Eat up," it grinned. "Remember: the one who finishes first is the winner."

"What ... what's the prize?" whispered the boy.

The troll leaned across to him with a very nasty leer. "Don't you know anything about troll customs?" it said. "The prize is – the winner eats the loser for pudding!"

The boy felt faint, but he swallowed bravely and made himself try very hard to think of a way to escape.

"Ready ...?" said the troll. "Steady ...?"

Suddenly the boy thought of a brilliant plan. Quickly he pulled his backpack round so that it was balanced over his stomach.

"Go!" shouted the troll.

They both picked up their spoons and began to shovel the porridge down, really fast. While the troll put its share straight into its mouth, the boy opened the top of his backpack and dropped his porridge into that.

The troll eyed him over the top of its spoon. Soon the boy's bowl was half empty and his backpack was full. He put down his spoon, felt in his trouser pocket and pulled out his penknife.

"Hurry up," laughed the troll. "Wah-hoh! I'm going to win!"

The boy took no notice. He opened the blade of his knife and slashed it right across the front of his backpack. The porridge came spilling out. The boy put down the knife, picked up his spoon and shovelled a load more porridge into the top of his pack.

After a few more minutes, the troll put down its own spoon and patted its big, fat belly. It was blown up solid like a balloon that's ready to burst.

"Oof," it groaned, "I'm nearly full up. I can't swallow much more. How come you're still eating, boy?"

“Didn’t you spot what I did, Mr Troll?” said the boy. “Just cut your tummy open like me. Then you’ll have plenty of room for more.”

“Yes ...” said the troll, “I saw. But ... um ... doesn’t it hurt?”

“No,” said the boy quite truthfully, “I didn’t feel a thing.”

“Are you sure?” said the troll doubtfully.

“Oh, quite sure,” said the boy. He pushed his penknife across the table. “Why don’t you try it? You can borrow my knife.”

“Thanks,” said the troll.

Then the troll picked up the knife, opened the blade and slashed it straight across its belly. You can imagine exactly what happened!

“AAAARGGH!”

Very soon, the wicked troll was lying dead in a pool of porridge – and the boy was safe and free.

Once he had recovered from the shock, the boy scraped the porridge out of his backpack. Then he ran to the chest and filled the pack with the troll's gold, silver and jewels.

By the time he had finished, dawn was breaking, and it was light enough to see the path through the trees that the troll had brought him along. The boy trudged along it, through the forest and down the mountainside, dragging his heavy pack stuffed full of treasure behind him. He didn't stop until he reached his home.

His father and two brothers were standing anxiously by the door.

"Where have you been all this time?" they cried.

"Oh, I decided that fetching firewood was too boring," said the boy, "so I brought back a few other items instead."

He tipped his backpack upside-down so that all the glittering treasures came tumbling out.

His brothers and his father were flabbergasted. Not only was the boy braver than them, but he was certainly much more clever!

They begged him to tell them where the treasure had come from, but he just winked and refused to reply.

They were soon too busy enjoying their new-found riches to care. And ever after that, they always treated the boy with great respect.

How to make your own Trolls' Porridge

(enough for two)

Ingredients

- ½ cup of porridge oats
- 1 cup of water
- ½ teaspoon of cinnamon
- ½ teaspoon of ginger
- 1 teaspoon of raisins
- 1 teaspoon of desiccated coconut
- 1 dessertspoon of natural yoghurt

What to do

1. Put the oats and water into a saucepan and mix well.
2. Heat the mixture and bring it to the boil.
3. Turn the heat right down and leave to simmer for three minutes.
4. Add the cinnamon, ginger, raisins and coconut. Mix well and cook for another minute.
5. Remove from the heat and stir in the yoghurt.
6. Serve in bowls.

The Smell of Almond Cookies

The smell of almond cookies was fantastic.

Wong Li Mei was hungry. Really hungry. She stood outside the Rising Sun Bakery, inhaling the wonderful aroma of cookies baking.

She was on her way home from collecting firewood. Her family was very poor and couldn't afford treats like almond cookies. The delicious smell enveloped her as she lingered outside the bakery. Wong Li Mei laid down the bundle of firewood that she had been carrying on her back from the forest. She pretended that she was about to buy some of the cookies and take them home to her family.

She pressed her nose up against the window, but this wasn't close enough. So she edged over and stood by the open door.

Now the smell was so tempting that she couldn't resist going further.

She stood just inside the door, closed her eyes, and deeply inhaled the almond air.

"What do you think you're doing?" snapped a voice.

Wong Li Mei opened her eyes and was startled to see the face of the baker glowering at her. Sun Shen was a master baker who concocted the sweetest almond cookies in all the land. He was also a mean and nasty man who was rude to people like Wong Li Mei and her family.

"I'm breathing in the smell of your wonderful cookies," replied Wong Li Mei.

"So how many have you come in to purchase?" sneered Sun Shen.

"Sadly, none," responded Wong Li Mei quietly. "I don't have any money."

"So what are you doing in my shop then?" said Sun Shen, menacingly. "You've got a nerve, haven't you? Coming into my shop with no money. Who do you think you are?"

"I haven't done anything wrong," said Wong Li Mei. "Smelling's free, isn't it?"

"Not here it isn't." Sun Shen was furious. "How dare you come into my shop with no money!"

"All right," said Wong Li Mei. She was getting annoyed now at Sun Shen's manner. "I'll move out into the street and smell your cookies from there."

"Oh no, you won't," said Sun Shen, emerging from behind the counter. "I don't want you cluttering up the pavement. You'll get in the way of my customers. As for that firewood you dumped outside my shop, take it away at once. Smelling isn't free and never will be! Not in my shop anyway. Get out and don't come back!"

With that, he bundled Wong Li Mei out of the shop. On the way out they collided with a richly dressed man who was just entering the bakery.

It was Chung Wah, who owned one of the best restaurants in town. In the past, Wong Li Mei's mother had worked in his restaurant, and on cold days, Chung Wah had let Wong Li Mei and her brother warm up in the restaurant kitchen.

"Hello, Wong Li Mei," said Chung Wah. "How's your mother?"

"She's at home with my brother and the baby." Wong Li Mei was almost in tears. She was so hungry and the baker's harsh words still rankled.

Sun Shen remained standing there, looking furious. Wong Li Mei knew he wouldn't want to offend Chung Wah. The restaurant owner always bought his bread and cakes at the Rising Sun, and Sun Shen had the greatest respect for a rich customer.

"Give her my best wishes, and give my best wishes to your brother too," said Chung Wah.

"You're very kind," said Wong Li Mei. She took a last few deep breaths of the delicious smells in the bakery. Sun Shen lost his temper.

"Stop smelling my cookies! I want you out of my shop now. Don't hang about outside either. You can take that firewood home right away."

"Wait a minute," said Chung Wah. "She's not doing any harm."

"Of course she's not doing any harm, sir," said Sun Shen humbly. "It's just that my shop is so cramped and I'm expecting a lot of customers throughout the day."

Sun Shen rubbed his hands together, bowed low and began to grovel. "A thousand good days, Chung Wah. I hope you're in good health and that the gods give you a long life. May your purse always be full. May you–"

But Chung Wah interrupted impatiently. "That's enough, Sun Shen. You always have too much to say."

"A thousand apologies," began Sun Shen. "I would never wish to upset you. I only implore the gods to give you–"

"My usual order, please."

"Of course, Chung Wah."

"I have a rickshaw waiting," snapped Chung Wah. "Why don't you take my order out and load it?"

"I'd be delighted," said Sun Shen. "I'll load your rickshaw immediately."

"I'd better go," said Wong Li Mei. "I'll just take one last sniff of those almond cookies." And she breathed in deeply, inhaling the delicious aroma.

When she got home, lunch (what there was of it) was already on the table. Wong Li Mei sat down to eat with her brother Wong Lian, while her mother fed the baby.

"Any more of this corn porridge?" asked Wong Lian. "It's really good."

"I'm afraid it's all gone now," said Mrs Wong.

"But I'm still hungry," complained Wong Lian.

Wong Li Mei frowned at her brother. She was still hungry too, but she knew that her mother couldn't afford to give them any more.

"I'm so sorry." Mrs Wong was near to tears. "If only I could get out and do some work. I will when the baby's older. Then we can start eating good food again."

Wong Lei Mei sighed.

"That baker, Sun Shen, wouldn't let me smell the almond cookies today. He said I had to pay to smell them," she said angrily. "He told me to go away and not to come back."

"Sun Shen is the meanest man in the world," said Wong Lian. "All he thinks about is money. Smelling cookies is free."

Wong Li Mei nodded. She knew her little brother was right.

By late afternoon Wong Li Mei was so hungry that the pangs of hunger darted around her stomach like firecrackers. She had never felt quite so empty inside. She couldn't bear to sit around at home thinking about food so she decided to go for a walk to gather some more firewood.

On the way she met Chung Wah again.

"Hello again, Wong Li Mei. Still gathering firewood? I'm sorry that baker, Sun Shen, was so rude to you this morning." Chung Wah looked kindly at the little girl. "Tell me, Wong Li Mei, have you eaten today?" said Chung Wah.

"Of course."

"What did you have?"

"Corn porridge."

"Is that all?"

"Yes," said Wong Li Mei defensively. She felt the pangs of hunger bite deeper into her stomach.

Chung Wah thought for a moment. "I don't think corn porridge is sufficient. Let me help you out ... I know your mother can't get out to work and money is tight at home."

"We'll be all right," said Wong Li Mei proudly, as she hurried away. "There's nothing wrong. We're fine."

Wong Li Mei had not gone very far when she saw something glittering in the firewood she was carrying. She stopped and realised she was gazing down at a coin. Wong Li Mei couldn't believe her eyes.

The coin was a liang, which could buy a lot of almond cookies – and even some cakes too. "It is my lucky day. Fortune is smiling on me," she said to herself.

For a moment Wong Li Mei thought she should take the coin down to the police station. Someone had obviously lost it. Then Wong Li Mei remembered the smell of the almond cookies baking – the most wonderful smell in the world.

She picked the coin out of the firewood and put it in her pocket.

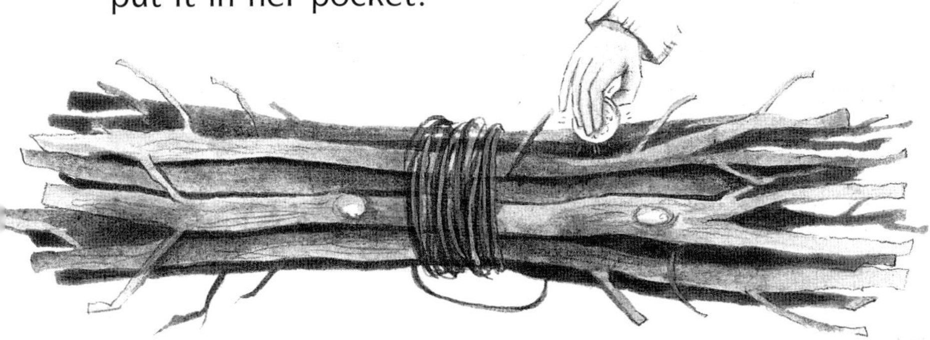

"When I can earn some money I'll pay it back to whoever's lost it," she thought to herself, and headed for the bakery.

As Wong Li Mei entered the baker's shop she smiled happily. At last she didn't have to be content with just smelling the cookies and cakes. Soon she would be able to taste them. Her mouth watered. She wondered how she would eat them. Would she crunch them? Or would she let them linger on her tongue?

Sun Shen spotted her immediately.

"You again! Get out!" he yelled.

"Why?" asked Wong Li Mei. The weight of the coin in her hand made her feel more confident.

"If you think I'm going to put up with you smelling my baking again, you've got another thing coming."

This time Wong Li Mei remained where she was. She fingered the coin in her pocket, turning it over three times for luck. She was looking forward to Sun Shen's reaction when he discovered that she actually had some money for once.

"I would like to buy some almond cookies – your very special ones – and some cakes as well," she announced firmly.

"I'm sure you'd like to buy them," Sun Shen sneered. "But what with?"

Wong Li Mei took the coin out of her pocket and put it on the counter.

For a second, Sun Shen's eyes widened with surprise, then narrowed with suspicion.

"Where did you get that?" he enquired.

"That's none of your business," said Wong Li Mei. "I have a whole liang. That's ten chien."

"Let me have a look."

Wong Li Mei showed him the liang coin.

Sun Shen couldn't believe that she could have that much money. But there it was. Sun Shen took the coin, polished it on his sleeve, inspected it, and finally bit it. He seemed satisfied and handed it back to Wong Li Mei.

"Very well," he muttered. "What do you want?"

"I'd like a couple of dozen almond cookies and four cakes, please."

"Give me the coin then."

"You give me the cookies and cakes first," said Wong Li Mei.

Sun Shen wrapped up the cookies and cakes and gave them to Wong Li Mei. "There you are then," he said and snatched the coin out of her hand. "Now push off!"

"But I need some change," said Wong Li Mei, angrily. "You owe me five chien."

"These cost you five chien and you owe me the other five," snarled Sun Shen.

"What are you talking about? I owe you nothing!" Wong Li Mei was no longer so confident.

"Yes you do. You owe me five chien for coming into my shop and smelling my cookies."

"You must be crazy!" yelled Wong Li Mei. "Give me my change at once."

"I told you – I'm charging you five chien for coming in here and thinking you can smell my baking for free. Good day to you."

But Wong Li Mei stood her ground. "That's stealing," she said. "You can't do that."

"I just did!" laughed Sun Shen.

Wong Li Mei was furious when she got home and explained what had happened.

"You can't let Sun Shen get away with that," said Wong Lian.

Mrs Wong was very angry. "Sit down right away and write a letter to the judge. He'll sort it out."

"Suppose the judge doesn't help us ..." Wong Li Mei said when she had finished writing.

"He'll do what's right," said Mrs Wong. "He's a fair man."

"He'd better be," declared Wong Li Mei angrily.

A couple of days later a letter came for Wong Li Mei from the judge, informing her to come to the court.

The next morning everyone gathered in the courtroom.

"This is the last case before lunch," said the judge. "Stand up, Wong Li Mei."

She stood up fearfully, her legs trembling like bamboo in the wind.

"You have accused Sun Shen of stealing," said the judge with a stern look.

"Yes," replied Wong Li Mei in a small voice.

The judge turned to Sun Shen. "Stand up, Sun Shen." Sun Shen did as the judge ordered.

"What is your occupation?" asked the judge.

"I am a master baker, sir. I own the Rising Sun Bakery. My cookies and cakes are the best in all the land, sir. You may have heard of them, sir, or indeed, have partaken of some." Sun Shen sounded very confident, and Wong Li Mei started to worry.

The judge turned back to Wong Li Mei. "Now, please tell me exactly what happened."

"It's very simple," she said. "I bought two dozen cookies and four cakes, and I gave Sun Shen one liang."

"And then what happened?"

"Sun Shen wouldn't give me any change," said Wong Li Mei.

"Is this true, Sun Shen?" asked the judge.

"I didn't owe her any change," replied Sun Shen. "She spent one whole liang."

"Wong Li Mei?" queried the judge.

"That's not true! The cakes and cookies only came to five chien. Sun Shen charged me another five chien for smelling his baking."

"Sun Shen? Did you do this?" asked the judge.

"Wong Li Mei had been in my shop earlier with no intention of buying anything. She just came in to smell my cookies. So I charged her five chien."

"What exactly is so special about these cookies?" asked the judge as he looked at his watch. It would soon be time for lunch.

As Sun Shen was about to answer the judge, he thought of a way to ensure that the judge acted in his favour. "It's a special recipe," said Sun Shen. "If you like, I'll tell you how I make my almond cookies."

"Well, be quick about it then," said the judge.

Sun Shen took a rolled-up piece of paper from his pocket and whispered his special recipe for almond cookies in the judge's ear.

"Try not to eat them all at once! It'll be hard – the smell is amazing, you know!" As Sun Shen described how to make the cookies, a dreamy smile appeared on the judge's face.

Take 75 grams of caster sugar, 80 grams of butter, 75 grams of finely chopped or ground almonds, 100 grams of self-raising flour, a few drops of almond essence, and one egg yolk.

Preheat the oven to 190 degrees Centigrade.

Cream the butter and sugar together. Beat in the egg yolk and almond essence. Then mix in the flour to give a smooth dough.

Divide the dough into 24 pieces, roll each piece into a round ball and roll each ball in the chopped almonds.

Place the cookies about 2cm apart on a lightly greased baking sheet and cook for approximately 15 minutes until golden brown.

Put the cookies on a wire rack to cool.

"If you're having lunch here, sir, I could bring some of my special almond cookies round," Sun Shen suggested.

"Well," said the judge thoughtfully. "If you want to bring some of your cookies ... "

"I should be honoured," said Sun Shen, looking very pleased with himself.

"Now, let's get on with this trial," said the judge. "Have you got any more to add?"

"Yes! It's the sheer cheek of her – thinking she can smell my baking for free!"

The judge turned to Wong Li Mei once again. "Is this true? Did you go in simply to smell the cookies?"

"At first," she admitted uneasily. "But smelling *is* free, isn't it?"

"You must let me decide that," said the judge.

Wong Li Mei began to shake with fright.

"What's going on?" hissed Wong Lian. "Smelling is free."

"Silence in court!" snapped the judge. "Do you have five chien, Sun Shen?"

"Of course."

The judge produced a moneybag from under his chair. "Please drop it in here."

Reluctantly Sun Shen put the coins in the bag.

The judge rose slowly to his feet. Then he shook the bag so that everyone in the courtroom could hear the money jingling.

"Do you like this sound, Sun Shen?" he asked.

"Money jingling in a bag is very much my favourite sound, sir," replied Sun Shen greedily.

"Are you sure?"

"Absolutely sure, sir."

"So. Wong Li Mei enjoyed the smell of your cookies. Now you, in return, have enjoyed the sound of her money jingling in this bag. That makes you quits, doesn't it?"

"But wait a minute," said Sun Shen.

"I don't want to wait a minute. It's time for lunch, and I'll take you up on your offer of those cookies."

"That was supposed to be in return for–" began Sun Shen.

But the judge had gone.

As Wong Li Mei and her family walked away from the court, Chung Wah caught up with them.

"Wong Li Mei, wait a minute. That liang you found – I think I must have dropped it when I met you on the road."

"Oh," cried Wong Li Mei, "I was going to give it back, honestly, as soon as I could earn some money."

"Don't worry," said Chung Wah kindly. "I'd like to offer you a job in my restaurant kitchen – you can pay it back that way. You can smell the food as much as you like. And when you've finished working you can eat some too! You and all your family."